160201

Richard Sanger

Playwrights Canada Press
Toronto • Canada

Playwrights Canada Press is the publishing imprint of:
Playwrights Union of Canada
54 Wolseley Street, 2nd floor, Toronto, Ontario, M5T 1A5
Tel (416) 703-0201; Fax (416) 703-0059
E-mail: cdplays@interlog.com; Internet: www.puc.ca

Playwrights Canada Press operates with the generous assistance of The Canada Council for the Arts—Writing and Publishing Section, and the Ontario Arts Council—Literature Office.

Canadian Cataloguing in Publication Data

Richard Sanger, 1960–
    Not Spain

A play.
ISBN   0-88754-551-3

I. Title.

PS8587.A53N67 1998   C812'.54   C97-932614-1
PR9199.3.S26N67   1998

Photo of Richard Sanger: Shane MacKay

First edition May 1998; second printing November 1998.
Printed and bound in Canada

Sie ahnten nicht, daß es nicht die Hoffnung war, die die Bürger Sarajevos höflich sein ließ (denn in Sarajevo über die Hoffnung laut zu reden ist ebenso unanständig, wie im Hause eines Verstorbenen vom Tod zu sprechen). Wir verhielten uns so, um den Besuchern nicht die Illusion zu nehmen. Und um ihnen zu helfen. Das gehört zu den alten Gebräuchen dieser Welt: Barmherzigkeit gegenüber Bettlern, Reisenden, in Not Geratenen zu üben.

They would never have imagined that it was not hope that led the citizens of Sarajevo to be polite (since to speak out loud of hope in Sarajevo is bad manners, just like speaking of death in the houses of the deceased). We behaved in such a way so as not to destroy the dreams of these visitors. And to help them. It's one of the old customs of our world: to practise charity towards beggars, travellers, and those in need.

Ivan Lovrenovic, DIE ZEIT, 10 September 1993

Production History

Not Spain was first performed at the Tarragon Theatre in Toronto as part of the 1994 Summerworks Festival. This full version was produced in 1996 at Theatre Passe Muraille in Toronto, and at the Grand Theatre in London, Ontario, with music by Peter Kiesewalter, set by Steve Lucas, and lighting by Martin Conboy.

Naomi Campbell and Deborah Lambie jointly directed both productions, with the following cast:

SOPHIE: Cynthia Ashperger

ANDREI: Arturo Fresolone

I am grateful to all involved, especially to Deborah and Naomi, for their help and advice.

The Characters

SOPHIE, a journalist in a foreign city, late 30s.
ANDREI, an inhabitant of the city, late 30s.

The Setting

A city in a war zone.

The play alternates between Sophie's hotel room and the building where Andrei has taken shelter; these should be suggested, not imposed. Sophie's room may comprise a chair, a suitcase, and perhaps a window. Andrei's quarters are larger, and everything in them is provisional: a bucket, a blanket, boxes for furniture, war-time debris, and a brass candlestick.

The scenes in which the two characters speak to each other all take place where Andrei lives; the other scenes are in each character's own quarters or in a neutral space.

The Music

"The Ballad of the Bridge" is an English-language verse adaptation of a traditional ballad story from the Balkans; it follows the plot of the ballad "The Bridge at Visegrad," adding a few details from other ballads and a fictional place name. (A full version was published in *Descant 94*, Fall 1996, with the title "The Bridge at Talar.")

Peter Kiesewalter composed original music for "The Ballad of the Bridge," which was used as a leitmotif through the 1996 production. In that production, however, Andrei recited, rather than sang, the ballad.

Peter Kiesewalter's music appears at the end of the play.

The Scenes

These scene titles are given to help readers; they should not be used or announced in production.

The Ballad of the Bridge
Flies on a Wound
The Pie
Carousel
Hello
Stories 1
Everything/Nothing
Candlesticks 1
Stories 2
Hello, Hello
Candlesticks 2
The Sky
Stories 3
A Song from the Bazaar
Stories 4
Jigsaw
Stories 5
The Guide-Book
Candlesticks 3
The Mexican Correspondent
Tell the Truth
Stories 6
Propositions
Not Spain
The End of the Song
Not Blood
Goodbye Presents

The Ballad of the Bridge

ANDREI *sings, as the lights come up:*

Three brothers are building a bridge;
King John, Count Mark, and George.
They are building a bridge at Talar,
There where the Duna roars.

Don't waste your time, don't waste your money,
Cried the voice of the witch.
You will never outsmart the river,
Never finish the bridge.

Flies on a Wound

SOPHIE Like flies...

ANDREI Like flies on a wound.

SOPHIE An open wound on the face of the earth.

ANDREI They come from all the corners of the earth.

SOPHIE A little gash that by chance opened up in one particular point, and spread, the place—who knows?—someone chose for everything to spill out so we could see what we are like inside.

ANDREI You know they're from the same tribe by their eyes, their eyes that seem so friendly, so interested, so compassionate, yes, but can't keep still—

SOPHIE We look at them, we try to see them but we can't, we can't look long. How can people live like this?

ANDREI They scan the background behind you just in case there's something there that's more alive, that's more to their taste, more succulent—

SOPHIE Look how quickly they discard everything that has no purpose, apartments, friendships, tractors; how they move from village to village, turning each one upside down to search for something of use, then—

ANDREI They feed, their eyes shift—

SOPHIE And they're off again.

ANDREI Like flies.

SOPHIE   Flies on a wound.

ANDREI   And they keep coming from all over the world,
the Americans, the British, the French, the
Germans, the Mexican correspondent—

SOPHIE   It happens like this: One appears, he looks just
like you or me, same jeans, same running shoes,
except that there's something about him that
tells you he hasn't used those shoes to play
tennis, or perhaps they weren't his to begin with.
He's restless, he bends over to pick something
up, some barely edible scrap—

ANDREI   They come in planes, in helicopters, in jeeps, in
armored personnel carriers; they come, swarms of
them, and some of them are women *(glances at
SOPHIE)*, and all of them bring with them bags
and cases full of up-to-the-minute equipment,
everything black and chrome and plastic—

SOPHIE   Just then another appears, to demand his share,
and soon there's a whole swarm of them, each
wanting a piece of that scrap, each believing it
must be good because there are more and more of
them wanting it.

ANDREI   Cameras with zooms and enormous convex
lenses, cellular phones, radios with antennae,
tripods with spindly thin black legs, and cables—
miles and miles of cables.

SOPHIE   And the more of them there are, the less human
they become, scrambling, scavenging, trampling
each other under their feet, willing to fight a
neighbour, a brother, over anything.

ANDREI   All that technology just to look at us. It's
almost flattering. And then their adjectives.

SOPHIE   Unfathomable, unprecedented, inconceivable,
atavistic, on a scale hitherto unimagined,
unspeakable.

ANDREI   But they'll speak, and speak as long as they have
             something on which to—

SOPHIE   So desperate they'll do anything—

ANDREI   To feed.

SOPHIE   To feed.

ANDREI   Or else they fly away.

SOPHIE   Or else they die.

The Pie

SOPHIE   The day I arrived, I was starving, I don't know
why. I went straight to the hotel to sleep, which
I hadn't done on the plane, nor the night before,
because there was a party in London. You see, I
met someone at it, I almost missed the plane. At
the restaurant downstairs, they were between
meals, but I couldn't go out, I'd just arrived. So
the waitress brought me something that looked
like pastry, that they hadn't eaten at lunch, and I
ate it right there in front of her. It was cherry pie:
very sweet and very red inside. Then I went
upstairs to sleep and I slept. I didn't dream of the
party or the man I've met or home. I dream of
myself, of my body and this thing inside me that
has put itself back together out of all the bites
I've taken, that looks like a map of somewhere
that shows all the countries in patchwork and
stitches, except that it bleeds at the seams.

Carousel

ANDREI   I see the road very close up for a long time. It's
chalky pale-yellow limestone, with bits of
broken cinder blocks and rock and a shiny belt-
buckle right near my nose and some broken black
plastic. Then there's noise—my neck hurts but I
look from the corner of my eye and then hide my
face in the road. It's four soldiers coming up the
hill behind me, with big boots that crunch, they
are coming closer, they are singing "Deux milles
à pied, ça use, ça use—" and just when the
chorus ends, one kicks me in the ribs. "Ça use
les SOULIERS!" UGH. And they march on.

Behind them comes an older man, with a crutch,
and he cries "Wait for me! Wait for me! I'm the
dead Goran's father! Wait!" But one of the boys
just throws a stone at him and says, "Get lost,
Grandad." And behind him I hear a woman crying
"You promised, you promised," but he doesn't
answer, and she goes by dragging two big
suitcases. And there are lots of people, they are
speaking and screaming and sobbing, and some
are dragging metal on the stones, but I don't see
them, I keep very still. And then it's quiet, and
far-off I hear a woman's voice singing an old
song from the mountains:

   Sings:

Three brothers are building a city;
King John, Count Mark, and George.
They are building the city of Talar,
There where the river roars.

I look and there's an old woman in a shawl
pushing a wheelbarrow slowly up the hill, like
she's in no rush, like this, going from side to
side. She is singing and at the same time talking
in a low voice to something in the wheelbarrow,
a baby or maybe an animal. But about ten yards
beyond me, she stops. Something has fallen
from the wheelbarrow. She picks it up—I see it's
an arm with lots of hair and blood and bone—she
looks it over closely, and drops it back onto the
road, and then she continues on up the hill,
humming that song.

     Sings:

They build the tower, they build the square,
The streets, the gates, the wall.
They build the city stone by stone,
And soon they've built it all.

Hello

SOPHIE	I had to get away, so I took a day off to visit a village in the safe zone. Tufa.
ANDREI	A little village two hours from here where I first saw the world—I hide my treasure there.
SOPHIE	I wanted to see the monastery, all the treasures the Crusaders had deposited there on their return.
ANDREI	When I go back it's always changed. Little things disappear like that.
SOPHIE	I went but I couldn't find it. I spent the day in the orchards with the cherries.
ANDREI	The store is empty, the café is boarded up. Now there is writing on the door. I enter.
SOPHIE	I was waiting in the square. The bus, I should have known, was late.
ANDREI	In the safe zone, I tell her, it is safest.
SOPHIE	There is no one in the square; no one but a dog and his shadow.
ANDREI	I bring her vegetables and cans and apricots for the children. We drink tea—there's no time, no place to make love. We laugh and laugh.
SOPHIE	I have a book and a bag of cherries I picked.
ANDREI	Suddenly I'm late. I rush for the bus.
SOPHIE	I'm reading and eating in the empty square. I look up.

ANDREI   There's no one—the bus I think has gone—no one but—

SOPHIE   There's a man running into the square.

ANDREI   There's a woman in strange clothes.

SOPHIE   A man I think I know.

ANDREI   She's reading a book.

SOPHIE   Or perhaps I don't.

                She faces him.

Hello.

ANDREI   Hello.

Stories 1

SOPHIE   I don't need much. I can get everything I need most places. A bed, a sink or shower to wash myself, a stove to make tea, and a desk to write at. And a book or two—whatever I'm reading at the time. I used to keep every book I read, I used to think I couldn't live without them, that I needed them to keep track of who I was. Then I came back from a trip and realized that I didn't miss them at all, I enjoyed being away from them. I could be myself, I could be someone else. So I had a big big sale, I cleared out everything, donated the proceeds, and swore to use the library. If it doesn't stay with me, why should I keep it? Travel lightly—write in pencil—pay your fines.

ANDREI   The apartment was on the ground floor at the back. It wasn't very big or bright, but we liked it because there was a courtyard where Katya and Boris could play. We left their toys out there, left the pram, hung our laundry. Then one day they hit the building, and Mrs. Santic's new TV landed in the courtyard. Azra left that evening with the children. That night I went walking in the city, there is more shooting and more shooting but I don't care, and when I get to my aunt's apartment I see flames on the horizon, something big and orange and glowing like a new planet I've never seen. It was the National Library. I've never been inside.

Everything/Nothing

SOPHIE	I have everything.
ANDREI	I have nothing.
SOPHIE	I have a lover, I have an apartment, I have friends, I have a name!
ANDREI	I had a wife and two children, I had an apartment, I had a job and a perfect happy life with family portraits on the mantelpiece.
SOPHIE	The human side of the story. That's what I do. They call me when they want it, and I don't say yes to everyone.
ANDREI	But there was always a little skull in the corner of the picture. And the skull said: "Everything is vanity."
SOPHIE	Now I wake up sometimes and ask myself: "Is this the name I wanted? Is this everything?"
ANDREI	I didn't know that my attachments to my family were also vain, that my love for my children was vain.

Candlesticks 1

ANDREI Nothing. No candle, no light, no match. Nothing but this candlestick. Once there were two. Azra noticed them the first time I took her to my mother's house. Up until then I hadn't really seen them—they'd always just been there, in the house, forever. When my mother gave them to us after we got married, Azra was so happy she cried. She said this made our house a real house now, that we were the rightful heirs and the candlesticks would carry on their journey through us. My mother told me not to tell her where they came from, and then muttered to herself: "In the house of the unbelieving, let there be a true flame."

Stories 2

SOPHIE   But I have to have a window. I always have to
              have a window, to look out on the outside world.
              Just so I know it hasn't gone away, and that the
              seasons continue in their lovely, mindless
              repetition. At home I'm spoilt—I have two bay
              windows that overlook a quiet square, where an
              old man in a jacket with gold braids sells the
              newspapers and a woman comes to feed stale
              bread to the pigeons at eleven every morning.

ANDREI   I went back with Petrus the next day, he's my
              neighbour, there had been more shooting and
              bombs and shells, and the building was
              completely empty—just Petrus and I and a
              couple of other men trying to load the biggest of
              our possessions onto carts. The televisions, the
              VCRs, a chest-of-drawers, and Petrus's deep
              freezer, which was very heavy and kept slipping
              off and which he wanted to take to his sister's
              villa because he had a feeling this was going to
              last a while.... I told him no, he didn't need it,
              now that Michaela and his children had gone. I'd
              left mine behind and was going to go back to
              eating dried sausages and cabbages from the root
              cellar, the way my mother and I had before I
              married Azra. But the freezer was very heavy, it
              was hot outside, and Petrus insisted, and I began
              to understand that the freezer wasn't empty.

Hello, Hello

ANDREI *is looking at himself in a*
mirror, or doing something likewise
mildly embarrassing. SOPHIE *enters.*

SOPHIE   Hello. Hello.

ANDREI   Hello.

SOPHIE   I came.

ANDREI   Who....

SOPHIE   You invited me to your house. I've come.

ANDREI   Oh yes. Of course.

SOPHIE   We were on the same bus back from Tufa. I had
gone to see the monastery.

ANDREI   There is no monastery in Tufa.

SOPHIE   That's what you said. I thought perhaps you....
At the roadblock, you remember, when everyone
got off the bus, that was when my camera
disappeared, and I thought perhaps you....

ANDREI   You are mistaken. I was not on this bus.

SOPHIE   You said I should visit you. You're Andrei.

ANDREI   Correct.

SOPHIE   I'm Sophie.

ANDREI   You're a journalist.

SOPHIE   Now you remember. You do.

ANDREI	I must give you some information.
SOPHIE	You see, when you invited me to visit you, I thought you were going to give me my camera back.
ANDREI	You want your camera— What do I know about your camera?
SOPHIE	But you took it, didn't you?
ANDREI	You know what they would have done? They would have shot you.
SOPHIE	Yes, yes. I know. That's why I really came—I wanted to, to thank you. You saved my life.
ANDREI	Hospitality is a custom in this country.
SOPHIE	Yes, it's one of your nicer customs, isn't it?
ANDREI	In every house, the biggest, the best room will be reserved for receiving visitors.
SOPHIE	For me, you don't have to bother.
ANDREI	No, no—the room must be nice for me. I am your host.
SOPHIE	But I'm happy anywhere.
ANDREI	It's the custom. And sometimes when we invite people it's just the custom too. The tradition is that we are always available. It is a shame, a disgrace on our house, if we let someone think that we are so poor or so busy trying not to be poor that we can offer our guests nothing.
SOPHIE	You are a very warm and hospitable people.
ANDREI	I say these things to help you in your visit. Because if we all accepted every invitation we received, and every guest we invited accepted our invitation, well, you see....

SOPHIE	It would be awkward.
ANDREI	Very difficult.
SOPHIE	You'd spend your whole lives inviting and being invited.
ANDREI	And sometimes it would be even worse. I would have to be a guest at my brother's, say, at the same time you were being a guest with me.
SOPHIE	And I would have to be a guest in three places at once. But we could all be guests and hosts together all the time—wouldn't that be fun?
ANDREI	So, to avoid this problem, sometimes we say yes, yes, of course, but we don't go.
SOPHIE	You didn't mean it. I'm so sorry. I didn't realize.
ANDREI	I say these things to help you on your visit in our country.
SOPHIE	It's hard to know everything.
ANDREI	But no one invited you to this country, and you came. That must be your custom.
SOPHIE	It's my job. I go where there's a story, something happening.
ANDREI	And you get paid. We make the news and they pay you!
SOPHIE	I'm sorry. I'll go—

A siren sounds.

ANDREI	Wait.
SOPHIE	No, I'm going.
ANDREI	You can't go now. It's the siren.

SOPHIE	I'm going anyway. It's not far. You don't want me here.
ANDREI	You must stay. Stay.
SOPHIE	But you don't want me here.
ANDREI	I have no choice.
SOPHIE	I understand you not feeling like guests. I live alone and there are times when I just can't see people.
ANDREI	Did you like Tufa? There are many things to see.
SOPHIE	I wanted to see the monastery.
ANDREI	The cherries from Tufa are famous.
SOPHIE	I know. I went for a walk in the orchards.
ANDREI	They have the best flavour and there are so many, so many that the branches sink with their weight and sometimes they break.
SOPHIE	No one had picked them. They were going rotten.
ANDREI	For this reason, when we want to say that there is a lot of something—
SOPHIE	I wanted to see the treasures—
ANDREI	When there are so many things you can't count them—
SOPHIE	All that gold and silver.
ANDREI	We say—
SOPHIE	What?
ANDREI	"Like cherries under a tree in Tufa."

Candlesticks 2

ANDREI The candlesticks came to my mother from my uncle who was—what do you call it?—the Bishop. When I was young, he was the only man I knew from outside the village—at first he frightened me, he was old, he had a long beard which he dyed, and his black robes stank in the heat. He came to stay in the summer and he brought presents. The whole village wanted to see him—and he, it seemed, only wanted to see me. I began to like him. The village was where he got away from all the important people in the city—but the people who thought they were important in the village didn't understand.

We would be sitting outside in the garden, and he would be telling me stories about the Knights of the Crusades and the battles against the Infidels, and sometimes my mother would come in and say there was someone at the door for him. My uncle would wink at me and say "Tell them I'm busy spreading the word." And then through the slats of the gate, I would catch sight of the mayor or whoever, who never came near our house at any other time, walking off slowly, explaining to his friends that the Bishop couldn't see them—even though it was the evening, it was August, it was the holidays, the Bishop was busy, spreading the word.

The Sky

ANDREI	You are enjoying your visit here?
SOPHIE	It's work.
ANDREI	Oh, I'm sorry. You are enjoying your work here?
SOPHIE	Yes, yes I am. Though it's difficult to know who to trust. Who to believe.
ANDREI	It is.
SOPHIE	The other journalists say you can't trust anyone. Ever. Who do you trust?
ANDREI	Not the journalists.
SOPHIE	What about your family?
ANDREI	No.
SOPHIE	Your wife and children?
ANDREI	Two children. Boris. Katya.
SOPHIE	What about them?
ANDREI	My family are dead.
SOPHIE	Oh. *(pause)* I'm sorry. I didn't know.
ANDREI	You didn't know them. Why are you sorry? You didn't kill them.
SOPHIE	I should go.
ANDREI	No.

Pause.

SOPHIE	I said I'm sorry because you must be devastated, because they're.... I didn't know them. But I know you a bit.... They died. I can't say anything, can I? And there's no use in you saying anything about them, because they're dead. That's it.
ANDREI	They're dead. That's all. It's simple.
SOPHIE	I should go.
ANDREI	Have some.... *(reaches in pocket)* What do you call this? Nuts?
SOPHIE	Sunflower seeds. Thanks.

> *They eat a few each, him spitting the shells on the floor.*

ANDREI	Like this. It's a custom.

> *She spits shells, some of which land on her dress or chin.*

SOPHIE	Shells—that's what they're called. We're spitting out shells.
ANDREI	It's a custom.

> *Pause.*

SOPHIE	I went to the monastery. With some Englishmen. It's a very beautiful place. Peaceful. *(pause)* Why did you tell me it wasn't there? I wanted to visit it and you told me it wasn't there. Why?
ANDREI	You wanted to visit the monastery? Just like you wanted to visit this country?
SOPHIE	It's a beautiful place. In other countries, you don't have—

ANDREI   And you don't have this war. That's not just a
monastery.

SOPHIE   It's a wonderful piece of Romanesque
architecture.

ANDREI   Do you know what they do in there? Do you
know what they tell the children that go on their
retreats there?

SOPHIE   That's not the building—

ANDREI   Those people are the building. They keep it
standing, they hold up the walls, the roof. They
keep the stones in place. I know. I did it too. I
went there on Sunday afternoons. My mother
spent the happiest hours of her life in their
chapel—or claimed she did just to get my father
angry. And her brother was the Bishop. My uncle
was the Bishop! Yes, the monastery is very
beautiful, the churches are very beautiful.... But
you know what would be more beautiful to me?
You know? It would be to burn them all to the
ground, starting with that monastery there.
That's correct. It would make me very happy to
see the fire rise and melt the lead in the stained-
glass windows, to watch those little coloured
panes fall out one by one and smash on the
flagstones.... Ping—there goes St. Sebastian's
halo. Ping—oh, St. Stephen's arm. Yes, yes,
smashed on those famous flagstones that the
Crusaders trod and that visitors from all over the
world came to stand on in their expensive
American running shoes.... And while all this
was going on, and the flames rose higher and
higher, you know what I would do? I would
round up all the people in the village, all the nice
faithful parishioners, and make them stand around
the burning ruin and sing "Hallelujah."
Hallelujah! That would be beautiful.

SOPHIE   Yes, and then what?

ANDREI   Then we would start from zero.

SOPHIE   But how? How?

ANDREI   We would look at the blue sky above us instead
of the dark church roof and the tortured stained-
glass saints. And I would remind the people of
the village that, in our language, the word for
sky is the same as the word for heaven, and that
we have only one sky, one heaven, and that's
what we would all believe in.

Stories 3

SOPHIE

And sometimes, sometimes, Lewis is there. Lewis. Louis. My lover. My paramour. My louis d'or. Not my partner, no. We don't live together. I don't live together well. Louis, my by-love, my for-love, my paramour. Now he wants a bigger part, he's got all ambitious. It's perfect the way it is, I tell him. I can be by myself, I can be myself, I can be unhappy when I want to. And I don't have to explain. And then sometimes, sometimes when I come home, he's there, he's let himself in and cooked supper for us, a surprise, say, asparagus, and I can forget everything and be happy being with him. Then in the morning, he goes down and gets bread from the bakery in the square and the paper from the old man—who speaks to him but never to me—and by the time we've finished breakfast and the paper the woman is there feeding the pigeons.

ANDREI

The freezer was full but I knew I couldn't ask Petrus what was in it, since he pretended it was empty, and I couldn't see inside because it was locked. But I began to get very very hungry just thinking about all the things in there. I remembered what dishes I had eaten recently in Petrus' house, I ate very well there, and at the same time I had to think how I could get him to open it up.... Petrus said since it was the heaviest thing on the cart, we should deliver the freezer first. I knew he was scared it would defrost before we got to his sister's villa. I knew, too, that if the freezer opened with Petrus and me there, Petrus would be obliged to give me a share of the contents. So I devised a plan.

A Song from the Bazaar

ANDREI	What about the Horse Bazaar? This would be a very good place for you to visit. It's in a suburb a bit hard to get to.
SOPHIE	On the other side of the river?
ANDREI	Yes.
SOPHIE	I thought it was called the Turkish Market.
ANDREI	Some people call it that.
SOPHIE	I've already been there.
ANDREI	It's wonderful, don't you think? You know this suburb used to be a village of its own. It was where they bought and sold horses and where the ironsmiths and leather-workers lived. Then when the Austrians were here, they taxed all the street-traders in the city, so most of them went to this village and the market got bigger and more variety. Now you can buy everything there, horses, leather, silver, carpets, birds....
SOPHIE	That's what everyone told me, but there wasn't much to see when I was there.
ANDREI	No?
SOPHIE	It must be the war.
ANDREI	I don't think so.
SOPHIE	What?

ANDREI	The market is doing very well now. Lots of people selling things, all kinds of things, their possessions, their family valuables. And lots of soldiers, journalists buying with dollars and Deutschmarks.
SOPHIE	I didn't see anything like that.
ANDREI	You have to go early in the morning.
SOPHIE	When I went all they had were rows and rows of cheap jeans and cassette tapes.
ANDREI	That's Saturday—it's the Young People's Market.
SOPHIE	There weren't many of them.
ANDREI	Then you went too late, I think.
SOPHIE	Eleven in the morning.
ANDREI	Much too late. Everyone has gone home for lunch.
SOPHIE	I wanted to find a carpet.
ANDREI	Of course. A carpet.
SOPHIE	But there weren't any, so I looked at the jeans and the cassettes, and I went into a café.
ANDREI	The café with the stained-glass windows?
SOPHIE	Yes.
ANDREI	This is very typical.
SOPHIE	They were very nice to me—they gave me some hot sausage to eat and some brandy to drink—I tried to explain I wanted coffee.
ANDREI	This is very late for them, you see.

SOPHIE	Then the barman understood and gave me coffee. And after he gave me another brandy and then another one.
ANDREI	It's the end of the week for them. They celebrate.
SOPHIE	And he pointed to a blind man in the corner. I took the second glass to him, while the barman yelled at him, and he started to play on his accordion.
ANDREI	Of course, of course.
SOPHIE	*(sings)* Three brothers live in a city....
ANDREI	No, no.

Sings:

Three brothers are building a city;
King John, Count Mark, and George,
They are building the city of Talar,
There where the Duna roars.

SOPHIE	It's a very beautiful song.
ANDREI	And very sad. It's about a bridge.
SOPHIE	A bridge?
ANDREI	Yes, it tells the story of how the bridge at Talar was built.

Sings:

They build the tower, they build the square,
The streets, the gates, the wall.
They build the city stone by stone,
And soon they've built it all.

All they have left is one little thing,
All they have left is the bridge.
They need a bridge over the river,
The river that laughs and sings.

> They start to build one morning,
> Before the sun gets hot.
> "A bridge is beautiful thing"
> Says John; his brothers nod.
>
> They know what beautiful things are,
> They have three faithful wives:
> Queen Margaret, Countess Anne, and Lena,
> Lena from the other side.
>
> Stone by stone they start to build
> Two arches and a pillar;
> By night it stands two horses high
> Above the silent river.

SOPHIE It's silent now.

ANDREI Yes, the river is sulking because the bridge is standing. Bridges are very important here.

SOPHIE Yes, yes, I see. A connection, a link, a bridge between places. Between people.

ANDREI *(standing up)* Yes, but the river keeps washing it away.

Sings:

> But the next day when they come down,
> Oh-oh! The pillar's gone.
> The river runs right past them and laughs,
> The river runs along.

Stories 4

SOPHIE Lewis had the magazine and was reading to me this long article about art forgery—how in these old European families, when they ran out of money the father would secretly sell off the original work and commission a fake from a tradesman to fill its place on the mantelpiece.... He did this very funny imitation of the excitable offspring swearing up and down and by all the most obscure Sicilian saints that this was the authentic Etruscan statuette they'd inherited, as a dour art expert shook his head in the corner. And while I was listening to him do all this, my eyes ran over the front section and there was this picture of these people lining up at some camp staring me in the face—the war had just broken out and they had a chart explaining which people were on what side and why they were fighting those other people.... And I said: "Why can't we live together?"

ANDREI On the way to Petrus' sister's villa, there was a little bar where we would go to drink beer after we played soccer. When we played soccer. I told Petrus I had to see the owner, Milos, about some business, and since we were going right by we could just stop there for a second. I went in and told Milos what I needed. We came out, carrying this big piece of calf, and Milos said:

"Petrus, I have no room in my freezer for this calf. Would you like it?"

"Yes, Yes."

"Good, let's put it in your freezer so it doesn't go bad."

"No, just put it on the cart. I want to eat it
today."

"You're crazy. You can't eat all this in one day.
Put it in your freezer."

"No, on the cart."

Like this, back and forth, and finally Petrus
opens up the freezer. It's full, absolutely full,
with food, with meat, with soup, with fishes,
with fruit, with ice cream even.

Jigsaw

ANDREI	Canada, Canada, Canada, Canada.
SOPHIE	I heard shells last night.
ANDREI	No, no, we have that every night now. Last night was normal.
SOPHIE	I thought I heard them over here.
ANDREI	No, it was the lower quarter last night. Tell me about Canada. Canada.
SOPHIE	What's it like?
ANDREI	Yes, what it's like....
SOPHIE	It's very beautiful. There are forests, there are lakes and rivers, there are mountains.
ANDREI	And what's it like in—in autumn?
SOPHIE	Oh, then it's especially beautiful. The leaves change colour, and they go yellow and orange and red, and they fall.
ANDREI	They all fall?
SOPHIE	No, not the pines and the cedars. But the maple, the oak, the birch, and all the other leaves fall to the ground, and they're bright bright bright....
ANDREI	Like cherries....
SOPHIE	Like cherries?
ANDREI	Under a tree....
SOPHIE	Under a tree in Tufa!

ANDREI	Really?
SOPHIE	No, no. It must be different. You should see it.
ANDREI	But I've seen the cherries in Tufa.
SOPHIE	But it can't be the same. You have to see it, see the leaves, the hillsides.... I hope you'll come someday.
ANDREI	No.
SOPHIE	You don't want to come to Canada?
ANDREI	No.
SOPHIE	Even if you could get a visa?
ANDREI	No. It's not for me. I can't.
SOPHIE	I could try. I know some people.
ANDREI	This was—is—my country. I can't leave.
SOPHIE	Why?
ANDREI	I can't. I don't want to go to Canada. I just want to know.
SOPHIE	Oh. Well, it's a very very beautiful country.
ANDREI	But you don't live in the forest. Not with all those beautiful leaves falling on you.
SOPHIE	No, I don't live in the country.
ANDREI	You don't?
SOPHIE	I live in a city in Canada. In Montréal.
ANDREI	Montréal, Montréal....
SOPHIE	It's a city in the country of Canada.

ANDREI	Yes, yes, there's a company there—they make very good puzzles, jigsaws.
SOPHIE	Really?
ANDREI	I have three of them. I had. No piece is the same—each one is different, not just different parts of the picture but different shapes for each piece.... Very difficult.
SOPHIE	You like jigsaws? You do lots of them?
ANDREI	Before. Then I would give Azra a new one every winter. We would work on it together. She loved it, but she would get so angry when she couldn't find the piece she wanted, she wouldn't come to bed. So sometimes I would make it myself with wood and paper, and hide it on the table and not tell Azra, and wait for her to see it.
SOPHIE	She didn't know?
ANDREI	I made very good pieces. Once there were too many pieces, one too many, there on the table, all by itself, when we finished the puzzle. I pretended this was the company's mistake.
SOPHIE	You cheated!
ANDREI	No, no. We know this problem here. A little mistake far away, someone forgets to put one little thing in a box—he's watching the girl in the window or telling a joke—and then the box comes here and we spend days trying to fix the damage.
SOPHIE	But they didn't forget the piece.
ANDREI	No, not this time. This is what I know Montréal for. Very good, very difficult jigsaw puzzles. It must be very nice, Montréal.
SOPHIE	It's peaceful.

ANDREI	You like, ah....
SOPHIE	Peace. Same word.
ANDREI	You like peace?
SOPHIE	Yes. Well, not always.
ANDREI	You're a writer—you need peace to write.
SOPHIE	Sometimes.
ANDREI	You have a good life. You're like some kind of people we know here.
SOPHIE	What do you mean?
ANDREI	You get everything you want. You get peace. And you get war when you want it.
SOPHIE	I don't want war. Nobody wants it. I came here because I want it to end. I want to help stop it.
ANDREI	And how will you do that?
SOPHIE	I will talk to people like you. I will find out what's going on here. I will write about it— write about what it's like to live here—about how people here need warmth, need water, need food, need hope.
ANDREI	*(as if trying to recall the source of her words)* Yes, yes, we know this song here. It's....
SOPHIE	And maybe if enough people read what I write, maybe they will understand that they must, and their governments must, do something too.
ANDREI	It's—it's Beatles. You liked the Beatles?
SOPHIE	*(puzzled)* What?
ANDREI	I did too. Such stupid, happy music.

Stories 5

SOPHIE

Lewis looked up and said: "Let's." It was a lovely spring morning: I had put daffodils in a vase, and there was bread and jam and coffee and fruit on the table. "Let's what?" "Let's live together," he said, and reached out for my hand. "I'll move in, I'll pay rent." I looked down at the newspaper and at the pictures of those people and their bombed-out towns. It seemed so obvious, lying there on the table between us like some carcass we were about to be obliged to come to terms with. So obvious I don't know why I needed to say it: "We'll fight."

ANDREI

So Milos went back inside with his calf. Petrus said, "When we get to my sister's villa, I must give you some of this food, I insist, but we'll leave it here for now and it won't go bad." We locked up the freezer and pushed it back into the road, which was now uphill and more potholes and stones. A shell exploded, I dove for cover, I saw the freezer on the cart like a big white coffin, Petrus was gone, and then, KA-BOOM.

The Guide Book

> ANDREI *rolling a cigarette.*

ANDREI   That moment you are on the bus, surrounded by people you don't know, the bus arrives somewhere you have never been, perhaps it's the station—

SOPHIE   Everyone gets off except—

ANDREI   Except you, and you sit there not knowing what to do, not wanting to ask anyone because they're all so busy, because you don't want them to know that you don't know where you are.

SOPHIE   And you don't know. It's frightening.

ANDREI   When I first came here the bus pulled into a shed—later I learnt it was attached to the station—the bus driver yelled something in slang I didn't understand, I sat on the bus alone, he yelled again at me, and I got off. And that day I walked out I was fifteen, I had just come from Tufa, all I had was my bag, and I was frightened, frightened that the whole city was waiting, just waiting to take this bag from me. When I asked people the way to the boarding house, they would say the names of streets and churches I didn't know. But I didn't dare say.

SOPHIE   You have to. I know—I feel that all the time.

ANDREI   And then this became my city. There are streets I walked up that first evening I later lived on, and buildings I saw then like fortresses or banks, which later became familiar places I entered to visit friends or conduct business. I made it my

	city, with my routes, my paths to work, windows I looked in, and faces I saw and nodded to.
SOPHIE	And now buildings are burnt and the windows are smashed.
ANDREI	I take a new route every day, I never know what I'll meet. It's the same for me as it is for you.
SOPHIE	We've both arrived somewhere we don't know, where—and we're alone. Why did you come?
ANDREI	What? I live here.
SOPHIE	Do you need a match?
ANDREI	What?
SOPHIE	A match, a light. *(gives him a box)*
ANDREI	Oh, that match. Thanks.
SOPHIE	What other matches are there?
ANDREI	I played soccer. We would have a match every Saturday.
SOPHIE	Ah yes, a game.
ANDREI	Yes, a match.
SOPHIE	Why did you come here from your village?
ANDREI	I had a job. A real job. In a printing house.
SOPHIE	It must have been interesting.
ANDREI	It was busy.
SOPHIE	What kind of books?

ANDREI	I don't know. I didn't read them. I set letters up when I started. And later when we got new machines, I worked on the pages.
SOPHIE	You didn't read them?
ANDREI	That wasn't my job. My boss said it's like a cake: Here we make the cake, we don't eat it. Make the book, don't read it.
SOPHIE	But didn't you want to know?
ANDREI	It was lots of writing. Words and words. Sometimes at night when I was trying to sleep I would see them in my head. Some of the books were for the church—my uncle, the Bishop, got me the job, you see. Menus for the restaurant too, and, oh yes, we did the city tourist guidebook with maps and all kinds of things. We printed it in English too. For the tourists and the relatives in America who come and have forgotten how to talk.
SOPHIE	*(pulling out a book)* Is this it?
ANDREI	Yes.
SOPHIE	It's a bit out of date.
ANDREI	Look at the maps. Look at the colours. Do you know how we—
SOPHIE	Lots of these places aren't there anymore. They're gone.
ANDREI	Yes... but they're in the book. And the book's in my head. There's the train station the Austrians built—see how grand and elegant it is—and here's the National Library.
SOPHIE	Which you never went inside.

ANDREI	Everything I need I keep in my head. See, on page sixty-two there is the river, the river where I used to go walking in the spring and the girls would wear their new dresses for the first time.
SOPHIE	They've chopped down the plane trees for firewood.
ANDREI	Of course, they would.
SOPHIE	And the bridge—
ANDREI	Yes, I know about that bridge. It is really very beautiful, that walk by the river.
SOPHIE	It's gone. I can't see it.
ANDREI	It's beautiful. The plane trees are reflected on the waves of the river, and the leaves float on the river's surface, drifting slowly under the—
SOPHIE	I should have come before the war.
ANDREI	You will never know how it was. There were cafés and long evenings and nights outside eating in the square. But you only come now, to see the rubble, to see the bombs....
SOPHIE	It's my job.
ANDREI	The barricades, the barbed wire.... It's not my city anymore.

Candlesticks 3

ANDREI   I was right. I should have been frightened of him.
He was spreading the word. He wanted me to be a
Bishop, too. He gave the candlesticks to my
mother when I was born. They came, he told her,
from a church that was burnt a long time ago, in
another village. Each time they are lit, he said,
remember that fire, those flames.

The Mexican Correspondent

>ANDREI *is evidently upset over*
>*something.* SOPHIE *enters.*

SOPHIE   You heard the news?

ANDREI   Tufa?

SOPHIE   I don't understand. It's a safe area. These people
are protected there by peacekeepers. For six
months they've been there and they haven't been
killed. They've survived. And today a report came
that they're leaving the village *en masse*.

ANDREI   Perhaps they think the safe area is not so safe.

SOPHIE   And it was a Mexican reporter who discovered
this. None of us believed him—we thought it
was propaganda.

ANDREI   People will say anything here.

SOPHIE   Then someone checked—and it's true.

ANDREI   Yes.

SOPHIE   All those people streaming out of Tufa, leaving
their homes and possessions, their whole lives
behind. It's crazy.

ANDREI   Stupid people.

SOPHIE   But what if they know something we don't, if
they sense it? Think of animals. Salmon finding
their way home to their spawning grounds, geese
sensing the onset of winter and setting off south.

ANDREI   No, no. They're like sheep. One person gets
frightened, runs away, and the rest all follow.

SOPHIE	But you're from there. You should know.
ANDREI	They're just frightened.
SOPHIE	Of what?
ANDREI	I don't know. I haven't been back there for a long time.
SOPHIE	That's not true: I met you there.
ANDREI	Oh yes, I went back once.
SOPHIE	And this reporter seems to know what they know as well.
ANDREI	It's a lot of stupid people from my village who don't understand. They don't trust the radio but they believe these medieval rumours.
SOPHIE	And you know what? He's one of the worst. He laughs, he makes jokes, he doesn't care. And he won't share his— You're shaking.
ANDREI	It's nothing.
SOPHIE	What is it? Tell me.
ANDREI	I can't ask you.
SOPHIE	Ask me.
ANDREI	I have a sister. You have friends.
SOPHIE	Go on.
ANDREI	My sister wants to know—
SOPHIE	She wants a visa?
ANDREI	She needs it very badly. I will be very very grateful.
SOPHIE	Is it just for her?

ANDREI	For her family.
SOPHIE;	Her whole family?
ANDREI	A very nice family. Two beautiful children. Perfect for Montréal.
SOPHIE	She's married?
ANDREI	Yes, she has a husband.
SOPHIE	Then she can't marry someone.
ANDREI	You must try. She's frightened of the war. The children are young.
SOPHIE	I'm not sure I can help.
ANDREI	Please.
SOPHIE	I'll ask. I will.
ANDREI	Thank you. Thank you.
SOPHIE	*(picking up a radio)* Where'd this come from?
ANDREI	A friend.
SOPHIE	But what about the blockade? It's a Japanese make.
ANDREI	He's a friend from the outside.
SOPHIE	Oh?
ANDREI	Like you, a journalist.
SOPHIE	What's his name? I probably know him.
ANDREI	Yes, you do.
SOPHIE	Tell me his name. Oh no. It's not him.
ANDREI	He visited me.

SOPHIE	He's the worst. I told you—the very worst.
ANDREI	He gave me a radio.
SOPHIE	You know what his stories are like?
ANDREI	I'm not interested.
SOPHIE	He comes from a country where the government slaughters people—he wants to pretend to his readers that this is normal behaviour, to tell them that here things are much worse. So they read his reports in the official news service, and pat themselves on the back and say: "How barbaric...." And he visited you.
ANDREI	Yes.
SOPHIE	And you took the radio he gave you?
ANDREI	It's very useful. Short wave.
SOPHIE	Are you sure you didn't just take it without him giving it to you?
ANDREI	What do you mean?
SOPHIE	I didn't give you my camera. You—
ANDREI	Your camera! What do I know about your camera?
SOPHIE	I just want to know.
ANDREI	You need a camera? Go buy a new one. And then get yourself killed.
SOPHIE	Is that what you live from?
ANDREI	He gave me the radio. He gave it to me.
SOPHIE	What did you give him?
ANDREI	We talked.

SOPHIE	He wanted something from you. What did you give him?
ANDREI	I gave him information.
SOPHIE	You told him about—?
ANDREI	Yes.
SOPHIE	How do you know?
ANDREI	I'm from there.
SOPHIE	Yes, and you go back there every now and then, don't you? You're my friend. Why didn't you tell me?
ANDREI	Because I told him.
SOPHIE	You don't think I'm a real journalist, do you?
ANDREI	No, no. I just didn't want to tell you.
SOPHIE	Why?
ANDREI	I didn't want to tell you more bad things about my country.
SOPHIE	But I'm a journalist. I need to know. Tell me everything.
ANDREI	You're my friend.
SOPHIE	Tell me the truth. Tell me.

Tell the Truth

ANDREI	There is writing on the door of the house in Tufa. I don't erase it, as I wish: signs of life, that might be dangerous. But what bothers me is I notice a mistake, I think, in spelling.
SOPHIE	Lewis wants to live with me. He knows me, he thinks, and it seems he wants to get to know me better. Ha!
ANDREI	Mr. Andric said there were mistakes in every book if you looked closely enough. If you want to find mistakes, you will find them; if you want to find something else, you will find that also.
SOPHIE	It'll be some wondrous self-forgetting nectar-sipping idyll, he thinks. All our best moments strung together and multiplied by two.
ANDREI	In most other ways, he said, books are perfect: They sit on the shelf happy beside each other, they don't want food or water, and they only speak to us when we pick them up.
SOPHIE	Logical flaw: Because we have been happy together, it does not follow that whenever we are together we will be happy—or that if we are together the whole time, we will always be happy.
ANDREI	I preferred people, and being together with them. But then everyone wanted to be apart, to be themselves, their true, their perfect selves. How hard it has been for them all these years sharing their houses, their streets, their villages. How cramped and unnatural they have become.

SOPHIE	Couldn't we just leave it at that? But it's never enough—there always has to be more. These two parallel lines, meeting each other so enjoyably at times, have to run on and on through the night vainly trying to merge, to become one, till they run themselves out, till they crash.
ANDREI	We never said, they never said anything was wrong—we knew each other, we thought, and what we didn't know was not important, it was just some quirk of table manners or decorative mark above the door.
SOPHIE	And there has to be more. More to have, more to know. What father did, what mother didn't do. The shadow falling across the delighted crib.
ANDREI	Now all these quirks, these little faults they found add up.
SOPHIE	Ah yes, the truth.
ANDREI	The mystery solved.
SOPHIE	The dark little secret that explains it all.
ANDREI	The truth about them—
SOPHIE	The truth about us.

Stories 6

SOPHIE   And so we fought. Look at them, I said. That's
nothing to do with us, Lewis replied, that's—
And he used a word, I can't remember what,
some phrase from the paper or such, that made
you think he knew all about it. How did he
know? He was like everyone else reading that
newspaper that morning—they were all judging,
making pronouncements, using words to label
the world. How could he be so sure he knew how
things would be, so sure that he knew me? There
are parts of me I don't know yet, little pockets of
resistance, dark corners. We fought, and then
both decided to think about it. I took the next
assignment I could abroad to mull things over;
and that, as it turned out, just happened to be
here. Right in the thick of it.

ANDREI   I lie in the road a long time and people stop
coming. It's dark and cold. I'm not frightened of
people anymore. I don't care if someone comes
and kills me. I just want someone to come. To
help me, to kill me—it's the same. And I lie
here a long time. And then there's a new sound,
something like an insect buzzing, one I haven't
heard in a long time—it's a motorcycle, a
motorcycle! It's Red Cross, Red Crescent, come
to take me to hospital. To the American
hospital! I know no one else has gasoline in the
city. The motorcycle pulls up, a man in a big
smile and sunglasses and safari clothes gets off—
he is very nice, very polite. He has a big black
box strapped over his shoulder, and he pulls out
this thing, I think first it's a new anaesthetic, it's
bright and shiny and he puts it in my face—it's a
microphone. He smiles some more and says:
"Are you dead yet?"

Propositions

ANDREI	You asked?
SOPHIE	I couldn't.
ANDREI	I told them you would ask. And you forgot.
SOPHIE	I'm trying to get hold of my friend.
ANDREI	Please.
SOPHIE	I can't promise anything. Where were you yesterday? I came to take you out for dinner.
ANDREI	What restaurant?
SOPHIE	To the Petit Europe.
ANDREI	I don't eat in restaurants.
SOPHIE	You weren't here.
ANDREI	I'm sorry.
SOPHIE	Where were you?
ANDREI	I couldn't answer the door. I'm sorry.
SOPHIE	You weren't here. The door was padlocked from the outside.
ANDREI	We must be very prudent in this city. Very very prudent.
SOPHIE	You were in Tufa, weren't you? What were you doing there?
ANDREI	I didn't go anywhere.

SOPHIE	You weren't here. Don't lie—
ANDREI	I didn't go anywhere. I tried to go somewhere. But the road is cut off now.
SOPHIE	What do you do there?
ANDREI	I visit.
SOPHIE	Visit who? Everyone left.
ANDREI	I visit graves.

Pause.

SOPHIE	I want you to tell me about your wife.
ANDREI	No.
SOPHIE	Please. I don't want to know how she died.
ANDREI	Yes, she's dead.
SOPHIE	I want you to tell me what she was like, what kind of person she was, what she liked, what she didn't like....
ANDREI	Why?
SOPHIE	I want to know about her, for myself. I want to know what kind of person you married.
ANDREI	She's dead. I married a dead person.
SOPHIE	She wasn't dead then. Pretend she's alive. I want to know what kind of person you would fall in love with.
ANDREI	*(sizing her up)* I see.
SOPHIE	So she's not forgotten. What did she look like?

ANDREI	I've forgotten.
SOPHIE	Don't forget. You can't forget.
ANDREI	I'm trying.
SOPHIE	Was she as tall as me? *(he looks away)* Was she this tall?
ANDREI	I don't know.
SOPHIE	Look at me. Please. Was she—?
ANDREI	I don't want—
SOPHIE	I need to know.
ANDREI	*(looking at her)* She was shorter.
SOPHIE	How short? *(hand at nose level)* This short?
ANDREI	*(his hand at her eye level)* This short.
SOPHIE	And her hair—was it black?
ANDREI	Yes, and longer than yours. And her skin was dark too. But her eyes were green.
SOPHIE	And was she...? *(hands signalling hips larger than her own)*
ANDREI	She was heavier, rounder than you. I made her like that. I gave her children. I gave her food. You are more beautiful, I think.
SOPHIIE	But you loved her—her roundness.
ANDREI	But she was more beautiful when I met her. More beautiful than you. Yes.
SOPHIE	You were very young then, weren't you?

ANDREI   I was seventeen. I was working but I went back
               to Tufa on weekends. Her father took over the
               hardware store there. Before it was a crazy mess,
               with boxes and boxes piled up on top of each
               other, with nails in one place and screws in
               another, with bolts in one place and the—

SOPHIE   Nuts.

ANDREI   The nuts for them somewhere else. Most likely
               spilled on the floor.

SOPHIE   It's a custom, isn't it?

ANDREI   She was there at the counter one day. I asked her
               where something was, she went to find it, and I
               followed her down the aisle. I noticed that the
               further she got from the counter where her father
               was, the slower and more interesting her walk
               became, so I came back and I began to ask for the
               things that were the furthest away—like rope,
               and wire, and fence materials. And one day it was
               cold but very sunny outside....

SOPHIE   You didn't need any more rope.

ANDREI   I had lots, all tied up in knots to make one long
               rope....

SOPHIE   And your tongue was tied in knots.

ANDREI   How do you know?

SOPHIE   You think women don't fall in love?

ANDREI   No, it was my, ah, intestines in knots. Because I
               went to the store just before closing and I asked
               if she would like to go for a walk. She was with
               her sister and they laughed. "A walk?" "Yes," I
               said. "Inside the store, or outside?" And so we
               went for a very long walk, except we didn't know
               how long it was.

SOPHIE	You should have taken a rope. Like what's his name in the labyrinth. You know....
ANDREI	I don't know this story.
SOPHIE	Theseus.
ANDREI	We didn't get lost.
SOPHIE	You know a match can be something else as well. If you have one thing, and then you have another one that's exactly like it, the second one is a match for the first. It's its match.
ANDREI	Oh, a pair of things.
SOPHIE	Yes, a pair of matching gloves, say. And people, too. If two people are very like each other or if they get on well, we say they're a good match.
ANDREI	So they make fire together.
SOPHIE	Yes. Yes. Andrei and Azra, it's a very nice story.
ANDREI	It's a normal one for here.
SOPHIE	I wish I could tell a story like that.
ANDREI	You don't sound happy.
SOPHIE	I have everything I want.
ANDREI	Are you happy?
SOPHIE	I have everything I want.
ANDREI	That's why you came here. You have something unhappy inside, you wanted to go somewhere where you can see the same unhappiness outside.
SOPHIE	I came here to do something, to help.
ANDREI	Do you want to sleep with me?

SOPHIE	What?
ANDREI	Do you want to sleep with me? Would that make you happy?
SOPHIE	I didn't come here for that.
ANDREI	Do you want to?
SOPHIE	No.
ANDREI	You don't want to? You don't find me desirable?
SOPHIE	No. I don't know. I'm thinking about Azra and how you met. You miss her, don't you? I know your heart stops but your body keeps on wanting food, wanting.... I'm silly to think you should stop—
ANDREI	Well, I don't want to sleep with you.
SOPHIE	What?
ANDREI	I don't.
SOPHIE	Oh. *(pause)* What do you want from me?
ANDREI	You came here. You found me. What do you want from me?
SOPHIE	I don't want to sleep with you. *(as if it had just suddenly occurred to her)* I—I want to interview you. On tape.
ANDREI	So you want a story.
SOPHIE	I want an interview.
ANDREI	Not today.
SOPHIE	No.
ANDREI	I have a headache.

SOPHIE	I'm sorry.
ANDREI	It's a joke. *(pause)* It is getting dark. You should get to your hotel.
SOPHIE	*(noticing candlestick)* That's very beautiful.
ANDREI	It's from the family. My mother gave it to me when we married.
SOPHIE	It's lovely. Where did she—
ANDREI	You won't find it anywhere. There's only one in the world.
SOPHIE	Such a beautiful candlestick....
ANDREI	But no candles. It's getting dark.
SOPHIE	Can we do it on Friday?
ANDREI	What?
SOPHIE	The interview.
ANDREI	Monday is better.
SOPHIE	Monday.
ANDREI	*(hesitant)* And my sister?
SOPHIE	I'll try again tomorrow.

Not Spain

SOPHIE   Do something. What? I try to sleep—I can't. I
go to the hotel bar. There are a lot of them
drinking there and laughing, all men, and the
young woman who gives them drinks looks
frightened. One sees me and comes up to me,
waving his arms and stamping his feet in a kind
of grotesque flamenco imitation, while the others
cheer him on.

"It's not Spain," he says and leers at me, baring
his awful British teeth.

"It's no holiday
Auden, Spender, Orwell, Hemingway
Fighting Franco
Writing poetry in the barranco
Throwing paper darts across the sand
Oh, this isn't no war for them—
This is a war for men."

Then he cackles and goes back to the bar, and the
others all buy him drinks.

The End of the Song

SOPHIE *and* ANDREI *with a tape recorder.*

SOPHIE   I called my friend in London. He's sending the papers.

ANDREI   He's sending them!

SOPHIE   The papers, the forms your sister has to fill out.

ANDREI   And then they get the visa?

SOPHIE   No—and then they decide.

ANDREI   How long?

SOPHIE   I don't know. It takes time. And they might say no after that. In fact, they'll probably—

ANDREI   They won't say no.

SOPHIE   They might.

ANDREI   No.

SOPHIE   Let's start. Once I've turned it on, I'm not going to stop it. OK?

ANDREI   Very good.

SOPHIE   *(pressing "start" and "record" buttons)* Andrei is a Christian, originally from the village of Tufa, who nonetheless believes the church is to blame for much of the bloodshed.

ANDREI   When I was a boy I wanted to go on a crusade. This is what the church taught me—to be a crusader.

SOPHIE	And now?
ANDREI	Is it bad to be a crusader? Is this what you think?
SOPHIE	But hasn't the church contributed to the violence by encouraging this intolerance, this animosity? You yourself told me—
ANDREI	The church teaches what it must. If you are a Christian, you cannot question it. You can only pray for the people who are dead. Perhaps that is necessary.
SOPHIE	Your wife and children were killed. Do you feel that was necessary?
ANDREI	In war many things we don't understand become necessary.
SOPHIE	Do you really believe that—
ANDREI	You want me to say that everything we do here is wrong?
SOPHIE	Killing people isn't very good, is it?
ANDREI	You want me to tell you that the way you live is right, the way we live is wrong, and that if we are more like you, everything will be right.
SOPHIE	I just want this to stop.
ANDREI	*(turning off tape recorder)* So do I.
	Pause.
SOPHIE	I thought because of your wife you thought differently, you thought—
ANDREI	I changed my mind.
SOPHIE	So you did. *(getting ready to leave)* I suppose that's all.

ANDREI	Yes. You're going soon.
SOPHIE	Next week. I'll come by before with the papers to fill out.
ANDREI	Have you found your carpet yet? You should go to the market again. Before you leave.
SOPHIE	But I don't want anything.
ANDREI	There are all kinds of treasures there. Have a look. Go earlier—before they pull out the brandy.
SOPHIE	I have so many things—I don't need anything.
ANDREI	There are lots of very old and very beautiful things. Family heirlooms, silver, china vases, the antique carpets that mothers gave their daughters when they got married....
SOPHIE	Really?
ANDREI	They call it the Vultures' Market now.
SOPHIE	I thought it was the Horses'.
ANDREI	Now it's the Vultures'. Everything they sell comes from the dead, from people who have been killed, that's why it's so good.
SOPHIE	I'm not a vulture. I can't buy something that belonged to someone.
ANDREI	Why not? Anything really old belonged to someone else before. Why do you feel so guilty about your money? Spend it, enjoy it. You can find something very old and very beautiful to take home, and you don't have to know where it came from and what it meant. You can imagine that.
SOPHIE	I don't want anything.

ANDREI   You wanted a carpet.

SOPHIE   I wanted... I want something special.

ANDREI   You could have a wonderful antique Persian
                carpet the colour of the cherries in Tufa, for
                nothing. For a song.

SOPHIE   For what?

ANDREI   For a song. I like that expression. I sing a
                song—you give me something.

SOPHIE   But you never—

ANDREI   I did sing you a song.

SOPHIE   You never finished it. There is a bridge at Talar,
                you know.

ANDREI   Of course, there is.

SOPHIE   You said the bridge keeps getting washed away
                by the river. But, in the end, the bridge got built.
                It must have because there is a bridge there now,
                a very old one.

ANDREI   I'll tell you the end.

SOPHIE   I want you to sing it to me.

ANDREI   It's very sad. I can't.

SOPHIE   But it's about building a bridge, a connection,
                that still stands today.

ANDREI   The three brothers go to the old woman of the
                hill, who is like a witch, and ask for her help to
                finish the bridge.

                                    Sings:

Don't waste your time, don't waste your money
Cried the voice of the witch.
You will never outsmart the river,
Never finish the bridge.

Never?—Not in a thousand years,
Unless your wives are true,
And you wall one up in a pillar,
That way the bridge won't move.

They must bury her in the pillar. That way the
bridge will be faithful too. So the three brothers
all promise not to tell their wives, they swear to
leave it to chance which one will come. But that
night each of them goes to his wife and watches
her with sad eyes. They go to bed: I can't tell
you the things they did there, or what they might
have said. But the next morning, it happens that
the wives of the two older brothers are sick and
ask Lena to go.

SOPHIE   Their husbands told them!

ANDREI   *Sings:*

I'd be happy to go, said Lena,
And do as you request.
But I have all this linen to wash
And a baby at my breast.

Oh, I'll take care of him, said Margaret,
I'll wash your sheets, said Anne.
Lena put on her best white dress,
To take lunch to the men.

His brothers smiled to see her come
But George, her husband, cried.
She looked more beautiful than ever,
Lena from the other side.

Why is your face so wet? she asked.
Why do you look so sad?
I've brought you rabbit for lunch, my love,
Rabbit and wine and bread.

SOPHIE   She thinks she's safe.

ANDREI   *Sings:*

Stone by stone the masons wall her up,
Beginning at the toes.
At first she thinks it's just a joke,
A joke that grows and grows.

At her knees, it's stopped being funny.
At her hips, she calls for George.
At her waist, she begs for mercy,
But her voice is growing hoarse.

At her breast the masons take pity,
And leave her two small holes.
Two holes to suckle her son through.
They leave, and lay the next row.

Up and up the pillar rises,
Past her neck, past her crown.
The next morning a new bridge stands,
But Lena's voice is gone.

Not Blood

SOPHIE   I gave away the books and things that were me.
Those that are me I left behind. I'm going back
to them soon, but even they seem far away, like
the apartment I'll return to, renewed and less
forgiving, like a student returning home.... There
will be a knock at the door and Lewis will want
in, to move in, merely to discover that I am not
what he thought I was. If only we could live
together. We can't. But let's imagine we could.
There will be a knock. "No," I'll say. "Don't
come in. Let's go out." The world flows through
me and I don't know it, don't know what secrets,
what flaws run through me.... Not blood—you
see, I don't even know what one month does to
my body, to me, what other sorrows I'll miss.

I know this. Before I leave, I will go to Tufa, not
to the monastery, but to the cherry orchards, to
walk among the trees and imagine how they
must look in season, and how the cherries must
fall, how like the thick red carpets in the bazaar.
They fall, and no one cares or knows how or
when exactly or what particular branch they fell
from. They fall and all we say is they were
many, they were red, they were sweet.

Goodbye Presents

> ANDREI *is rearranging the boxes, so*
> *that* SOPHIE, *who has just arrived, will*
> *have somewhere to sit.*

ANDREI   Excuse me. It was close last night.

SOPHIE   What was?

ANDREI   You didn't hear?

SOPHIE   Oh, the shells.

ANDREI   One landed right at the corner. I put this here so
the glass wouldn't hit me when the window
exploded.

SOPHIE   I'm sorry—I've got used to them.

ANDREI   And now you're leaving.

SOPHIE   What will happen?

ANDREI   I didn't think it could be worse. It can. I'm very
worried for my—my sister's family.

SOPHIE   Look, I brought you the papers. I've signed
them, so if there are any questions, they can
contact me.

ANDREI   *(accepting it)* I'm very grateful.

SOPHIE   Thank you for the interview. I did use it, even
though I didn't expect you to be so—

ANDREI   Things are very complex. You can't tell everyone
what happens.

Pause.

SOPHIE	*(suddenly)* Is Azra still alive? Is your family alive? The visa is for her, isn't it?
ANDREI	I can't tell everyone. I have to protect—
SOPHIE	Are they?
ANDREI	I can't tell you.
SOPHIE	They are. I know. You lied to me, didn't you?
ANDREI	I lied? No, no—I tried to survive.
SOPHIE	I trusted you and you lied to me. You realize if the other journalists find out, my name will be ruined.
ANDREI	And my family.
SOPHIE	What?
ANDREI	If they find out about them—
SOPHIE	What?
ANDREI	They'll be killed.
SOPHIE	I'm sorry. Where are they?
ANDREI	I can't tell you.
SOPHIE	I know. They're in Tufa. And they can't go out and you can't visit now and all they can do is wait.
ANDREI	It's a safe zone.
SOPHIE	But all those people were leaving.
ANDREI	Not them. I told them not to. I told them it's safe.

SOPHIE	And now you got the papers for them.
ANDREI	Thank you.
SOPHIE	I wish you'd told me. Then I could have—
ANDREI	That's not what you wanted.
SOPHIE	I wanted you to lie to me?
ANDREI	A story, the front page, a headline, news!
SOPHIE	I wanted the truth.
ANDREI	Otherwise you talk to someone else.
SOPHIE	I wanted to talk to you.
ANDREI	You wanted news.
SOPHIE	About the war.
ANDREI	About the death of my wife, my children.
SOPHIE	Your family aren't dead.
ANDREI	But I talked about their death. *(smiles)* For you.
SOPHIE	Yes, you did. Thank you.
ANDREI	You did your job, and I helped you. And now you're going....

Pause.

SOPHIE	Yes. Thank you for being my friend here.
ANDREI	It's nothing. Hospitality is our custom.
SOPHIE	Yes, it is.
ANDREI	Did you go back to the bazaar?

SOPHIE	Actually, I've just been there.
ANDREI	Did you get a carpet?
SOPHIE	Not a carpet.
ANDREI	No.... A painting?
SOPHIE	No.
ANDREI	Some china for your friend Lewis?
SOPHIE	No, it's for me, for my dining room table.
ANDREI	Let me think.
SOPHIE	It's beautiful and old.
ANDREI	Show me.
SOPHIE	It's just like yours. *(revealing a candlestick)* Look!
ANDREI	*(seizing it)* No, no, no, no!
SOPHIE	What?
ANDREI	It's Azra's! I gave it to her when I left.
SOPHIE	I found it in the bazaar.
ANDREI	They've got her! And Katya and Boris too!

> He hands both candlesticks to SOPHIE,
> who accepts them silently, and then
> walks away from her, mumbling.

ANDREI	Dear father, what I most loved, you have taken from me. It was dark, I did not see you, so I asked you to speak. You spoke and said: "Everything is vanity." Azra, Katya, Boris— vain, vain, vain. Take this one too, I say, take them both. And in the house of the unbelieving....

SOPHIE *(overlapping* ANDREI's *last sentence)* And in the square there is an old man who sells newspapers, and at eleven a woman comes to feed stale bread to the pigeons. How can I know what the paper doesn't say? How or when exactly or what particular people died waiting for that bread? Tonight Lewis is coming for dinner and I'm cooking. Wine, bread, pasta, salad, candles, candlesticks—I have everything.

Blackout.

The Ballad of the Bridge

Music © Peter Kiesewalter
Lyrics © Richard Sanger

Richard Sanger was born in 1960, grew up mainly in Ottawa and, after ten years in Europe, moved to Toronto in 1987. His poems have appeared in many publications in Canada, Britain, and the States, including *Descant*, *Queen's Quarterly*, *South-West Review*, *The Times Literary Supplement*, and in the volume *Shadow Cabinet* (Vehicule Press, 1996), nominated for the 1996 Gerald Lampert Award. He has also written essays and reviews for *Books in Canada*, *The Globe and Mail*, and the *TLS*, and has taught at the University of Toronto. *Not Spain* was shortlisted for a 1995 Chalmers Award. He has since written a new play, *Two Words for Snow*. He lives in Toronto with his wife and son, and is the 1998-1999 Writer-in-Residence at the University of New Brunswick.